Life Cycles

Richard Spilsbury

WAYLAND

First published in paperback in 2015 by Wayland
Copyright © Wayland 2015

Wayland, an imprint of Hachette Children's Group
Part of Hodder & Stoughton
Carmelite House, 50 Victoria Embankment, London EC4Y 0DZ

Produced for Wayland by Calcium

Editors: Sarah Eason and Leon Gray
Editor for Wayland: Julia Adams
Designer: Paul Myerscough
Illustrator: Geoff Ward
Picture researcher: Maria Joannou
Consultant: Michael Scott OBE

Dewey number: 571.8-dc22
ISBN 978 0 7502 9656 4
10 9 8 7 6 5 4 3 2 1

MIX
Paper from
responsible sources
FSC® C104740
FSC
www.fsc.org

Printed in China

Every attempt has been made to clear copyright. Should there be any inadvertent omission please apply to the publisher for rectification. The author and publisher would like to thank the following for allowing their pictures to be reproduced in this publication:

Cover photograph: Shutterstock/Vishnevskiy Vasily.
Interior photographs: Corbis: Jan-Peter Kasper/EPA 29b; Istockphoto: Don Wilkie 7b; Photolibrary: Tobias Bernhard 23; Shutterstock: 14, Victoria Alexandrova 7t, John A. Anderson 26, Noam Armonn 21, Benjaminet 33b, Henk Bentlage 5, 38, Ryan M. Bolton 31t, Cbpix 27, Vasyl Dudenko 34, Constant 43, Elnur 13, Errni 11t, Andrzej Gibasiewicz 17b, Fivespots 33t, 35b, 45, Eric Isselée 41, Jeya 22t, Sebastian Kaulitzki 10, Cathy Keifer 3, 20, Herbert Kratky 40, Willie Linn 9, Timothy Craig Lubcke 37t, Xavier Marchant 32, Mirrormere 31b, Thomas Mounsey 28, NatUlrich 39t, Anette Linnea Rasmussen 4, 17t, Sahua D 11b, Kristian Sekulic 39b, Serg64 16, Natalia Sinjushina & Evgeniy Meyke 8, Carolina K. Smith, M.D. 21b, Kristin Smith 19b, Specta 22b, Wolfgang Staib 6, Vladislav Susoy 29t, Tap10 37b, Mary Terriberry 15, Darlene Tompkins 25, Ismael Montero Verdu 19t, WizData, inc 35t.

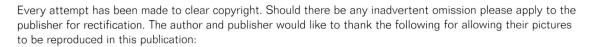

An Hachette UK company   www.hachette.co.uk   www.hachettechildrens.co.uk

SAFETY NOTE: The activities in this book are intended for children. However, we recommend adult supervision at all times as neither the Publisher nor the author can be held responsible for any injury.

Contents

CHAPTER 1

What is a life cycle?

A life cycle is all the stages of development of an organism. An organism is born, grows into an adult that can produce its own offspring and finally dies. When an organism dies, it rots away. The nutrients locked up inside its body are released, providing food for other organisms to continue their life cycles.

Start to finish

Every life cycle begins when an organism is born, hatches from an egg or sprouts from a plant seed. The young organism faces a number of threats early on in its life. It may be eaten by a predator or get too hot or too cold. If it escapes these dangers, the young organism will grow into an adult. The adult is bigger and stronger and better able to survive in its habitat. Growth also ensures the development of abilities such as running and finding food.

Most plants continue to grow, often slowly, throughout their lifetime.

The key part of every organism's life cycle is reproduction. This is when an organism produces young of its own. An organism such as a frog produces tadpoles that grow into new frogs to take the place of the parents when they die. This is essential for the survival of the species (one type of organism).

Some organisms grow more quickly than others and at different rates during their lives. Most animals grow very rapidly when they are young, but stop growing as adults.

Tadpoles hatch from eggs and slowly change into adult frogs. This process is called metamorphosis.

A female elephant gives birth to her calf about 22 months after mating with a male elephant.

Eventually, every living organism will die. The time from birth to death varies widely between different species. After death, organisms including bacteria break down dead bodies and release nutrients into the soil for other organisms to use.

Embryos

Embryos usually develop inside an egg or seed and then emerge as young organisms that live independent lives. Eggs range in size from tiny insect eggs to enormous ostrich eggs. Seeds range in size from microscopic orchid seeds to coconuts. Eggs and seeds protect and supply nutrients to the developing embryo. In eggs, the nutrient store is the yolk. In seeds, it is the endosperm. Many animals, including people, develop from egg cells that grow inside their mother's body.

Conifer cones contain seeds that grow into new conifer trees.

BEARING YOUNG

Big animals can be divided into two main reproductive groups. One group gives birth to live young. They are called live-bearing, or viviparous, animals. The second group lays eggs that eventually hatch into young animals. They are called egg-laying, or oviparous, animals.

How organisms grow

Cells are the tiny building blocks of every living thing. An embryo grows by increasing the number of cells in its body. One cell divides into two cells, and each of these smaller, identical cells increases in size. Then the two cells divide into four, four into eight and so on. As the number of cells increases, some cells also start to differentiate. They become different types of cells that do different jobs. For example, some animal cells become muscle tissue that helps the animal move.

The instructions about how cells should divide and differentiate are contained within genes. Genes are made from sequences of a complex chemical called deoxyribonucleic acid (DNA).

Some organisms are complex or made up of many cells. The world's biggest living things, blue whales and giant redwood trees, consist of billions of cells grouped into many different tissues. An adult person is made up of around 100 billion cells. Simple organisms, such as amoebas, consist of just one cell.

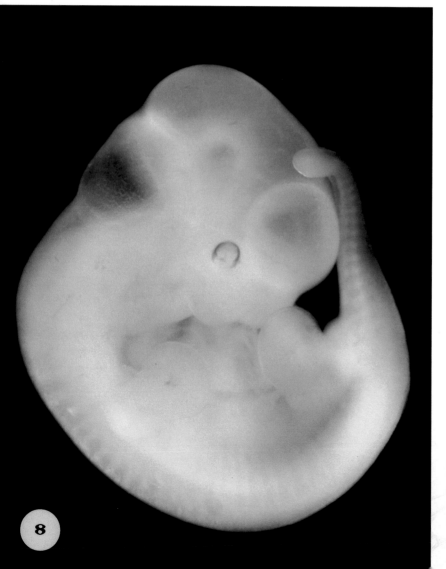

Food for fuel

Every living thing needs food to grow and develop. The cells in an organism's body break down food to release the energy needed for growth, development and repair. Plants produce their own food in a process called photosynthesis. They also take in nutrients from the soil. Animals are consumers. They consume, or feed on, plants or other animals to get their nutrients.

A mouse develops from a fertilised egg. After 11 days, the egg has grown into an embryo showing features such as a head and tail.

An osprey catches fish as food to fuel its own growth but also that of its chicks. Without this parental care, the chicks could not pass through their life stages to adulthood.

Life stages

From the moment they are born, some young organisms look like smaller versions of their parents. Others change dramatically as they develop into an adult. The trunk or stem of a young sapling is slender and flexible.

As a mature tree, the stem is solid, straight and unbending. A young frog is called a tadpole. It has no legs and breathes underwater. An adult frog has four legs and breathes in oxygen from the air. Not all organisms go through such dramatic changes.

INVESTIGATE:
Water and life

YOU WILL NEED:
2 plant pots, water

The bodies of most animals and plants are made up of water. Why is this tasteless, invisible liquid so important to an organism's life cycle? Find out in this investigation. Take two small pot plants, such as geraniums, which you can grow from seed or buy. Water just one of the plants each day, but keep both pots in a sunny place. Record the growth of each plant. What happens to the plant that does not get any water? How does this compare to the plant that receives water?

Reproduction

Most animals and plants reproduce sexually. The male produces male sex cells. In animals, the sex cells are usually called sperm. In plants, they are usually called pollen. The female produces sex cells called eggs.

During sexual reproduction, the sperm or pollen may join with, or fertilise, an egg. Some organisms mate so the sperm and egg can join up. Genes from each cell combine, and the fertilised egg becomes an embryo. The embryo has a slightly different set of genes from either parent. This variation may enable the offspring to survive better than its parents.

Some animals and plants reproduce asexually. They do not produce sex cells. For example, tiny freshwater animals called hydra develop as buds on the parent animal and break off to become new hydras. The new hydra is identical to its parent and has a matching set of genes.

Recycling nutrients

Some organisms die as soon as they have reproduced and passed on their genes to the next generation. Plants called annuals grow, flower, make seeds and then die within one season. A male octopus dies a few months after mating, and the female dies shortly after her eggs hatch. Other organisms may reproduce again and again over many years before they die.

Only one sperm cell can penetrate the membrane of the egg to fertilise it.

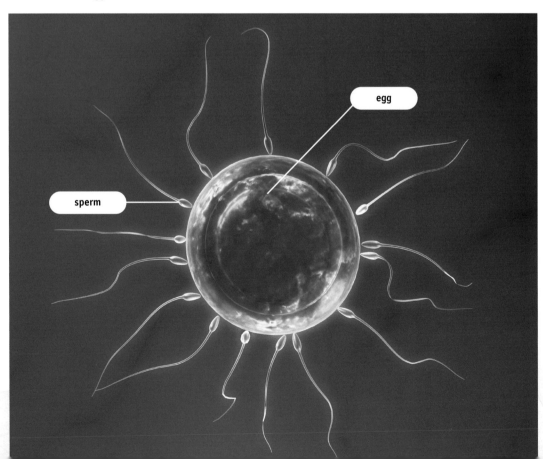

egg

sperm

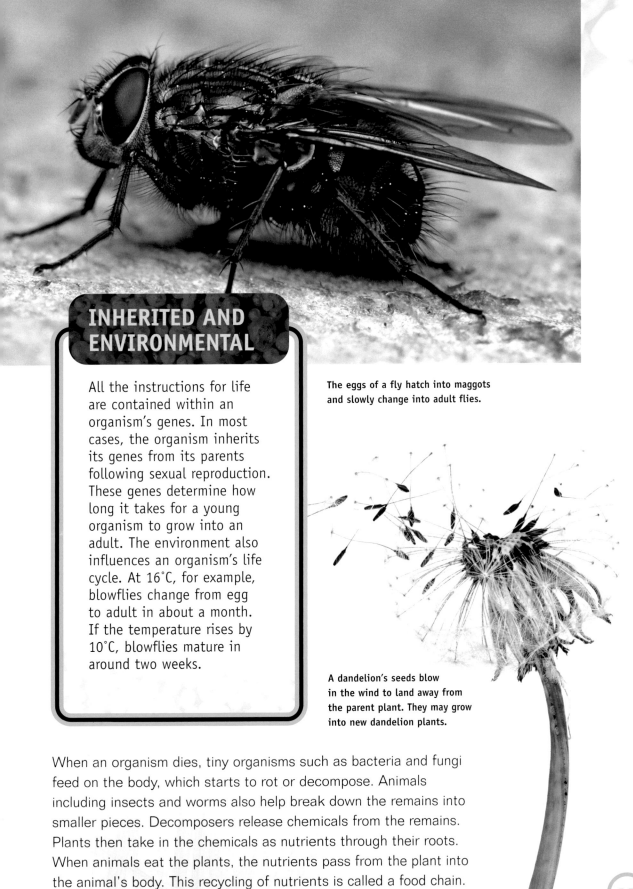

INHERITED AND ENVIRONMENTAL

All the instructions for life are contained within an organism's genes. In most cases, the organism inherits its genes from its parents following sexual reproduction. These genes determine how long it takes for a young organism to grow into an adult. The environment also influences an organism's life cycle. At 16°C, for example, blowflies change from egg to adult in about a month. If the temperature rises by 10°C, blowflies mature in around two weeks.

The eggs of a fly hatch into maggots and slowly change into adult flies.

A dandelion's seeds blow in the wind to land away from the parent plant. They may grow into new dandelion plants.

When an organism dies, tiny organisms such as bacteria and fungi feed on the body, which starts to rot or decompose. Animals including insects and worms also help break down the remains into smaller pieces. Decomposers release chemicals from the remains. Plants then take in the chemicals as nutrients through their roots. When animals eat the plants, the nutrients pass from the plant into the animal's body. This recycling of nutrients is called a food chain.

CHAPTER 2

Plant life cycles

Most plants emerge from tiny structures called seeds. They grow and develop into different forms using energy from food, which they make using the energy from the sun.

Most plants reproduce sexually. They produce sex cells in special plant parts called flowers and cones. Following fertilisation, the plants produce seeds that grow into new plants. Some plants produce new plants asexually, while others reproduce using both sexual and asexual reproduction.

What is germination?

The hard outer case of a seed protects the embryo and food store inside from drying out or getting damaged before germination. Most seeds can only germinate if the conditions are right, for example, if there are enough daylight hours or if the soil contains enough moisture. In the first stage of germination,

the seed case splits open. The young root grows out and down into the soil, using energy from the food store. Then the young shoot grows out and up towards the light, gradually spreading out the seed leaves. These are the remains of the food store fuelling the early seedling development. As soon as the roots take hold, the seedling develops leaves that can make food

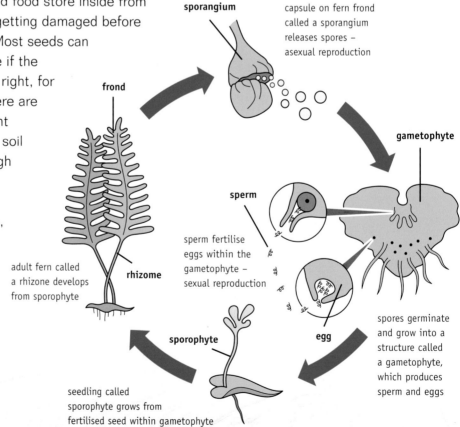

This illustration shows the reproductive stages of a typical fern life cycle – a combination of sexual and asexual reproduction.

frond

adult fern called a rhizone develops from sporophyte

rhizome

sporangium

capsule on fern frond called a sporangium releases spores – asexual reproduction

gametophyte

sperm

sperm fertilise eggs within the gametophyte – sexual reproduction

egg

spores germinate and grow into a structure called a gametophyte, which produces sperm and eggs

sporophyte

seedling called sporophyte grows from fertilised seed within gametophyte

by photosynthesis. The young plant then grows more leaves and a stronger stem to support the growing plant.

When a seed germinates under the ground, the seedling breaks through the soil towards the light and extends leaves. The seedling can then start to make food by photosynthesis.

How to grow

Most plants grow from points such as the tips of the leaves, twigs or roots. For example, cells at the root tip divide and grow to make the root longer. Trees grow fatter because cells divide just below the bark. Plants such as grasses always grow from the base of the leaves. This is why the grass on a lawn always grows back quickly after you cut it.

Plants of the same species grow in much the same way, but individuals grow slightly differently depending on their surroundings. For example, climbing plants such as the Virginia creeper follow the shape of the wall on which they are growing. Trees exposed to a regular strong wind from one direction will grow more on the side away from the wind, so plant parts such as the leaves will avoid damage.

FOOD FACTORIES

The food factories of green plants are the leaves. During photosynthesis, the leaves absorb energy from sunlight and use it to transform carbon dioxide and water into a sugar called glucose. Plants take in carbon dioxide in the air through stomata (holes) in their leaves. They suck up water through their roots. The plant uses dissolved minerals in the water from the soil to build healthy new cells.

Flowers, cones and pollination

The female parts in flowers are called carpels. The male parts are called stamens. Reproduction usually occurs when the pollen from the stamen of one plant's flower transfers to the carpel of another plant's flower. The pollen grows into the carpel and fertilises the egg inside. Cones are the reproductive structures on conifers such as pines. Pollen from the male cones pollinates the tough, woody female cones.

Pollen transfer

Plants rely on animals, wind or water for pollination. Flowers pollinated by animals are usually colourful and may have an attractive scent and sweet nectar to

THE REPRODUCTIVE ORGANS OF A FLOWER

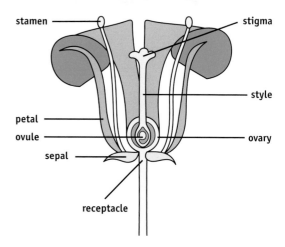

stamen — stigma — style — petal — ovule — ovary — sepal — receptacle

draw in visitors. When an insect, bird or bat visits the flowers to drink the nectar, pollen grains stick to their bodies. When they stop at the next plant, the pollen transfers to the sticky carpel and pollinates it. Plants that rely on the wind for pollination include conifers and grasses.

A bee picks up pollen as it feeds on the nectar of a lily flower. The insect transfers the pollen to a new lily plant when it stops to feed again.

Grass has dull-coloured flowers with small, or even no, petals. Moving air blows the pollen from flower to flower.

Asexual reproduction

Some plants reproduce without pollen. Some grow underground parts called bulbs and tubers, which act as food stores for the parent plant but can also develop into new plants. Strawberry plants grow long stems across the ground, called runners, which develop new strawberry plantlets.

Ferns reproduce using spores. These tiny grain-like cells are produced asexually on the underside of a fern frond. Spores fall from the fronds and, in shady, damp conditions, germinate into a tiny green heart-shaped structure called a prothallus. The fern can then reproduce sexually. A male sex cell fertilises the female cell on the prothallus, and a new fern starts to grow. Mosses also have an asexual stage in their life cycles. They produce spores at the tips of little stalks that grow above their leaves.

INVESTIGATE:
Spore print

YOU WILL NEED:
sheet of white paper, fern fronds

Collect a few fern fronds in the autumn, when the spores develop. You can tell when this has happened because you will see dots on the underside of the frond become grainy and darker in colour. Place a fern frond on a sheet of white paper with the spore cases touching the paper. Leave it on a flat surface overnight. In the morning, you should see a 'print' of the fern frond in the form of spores left on the paper.

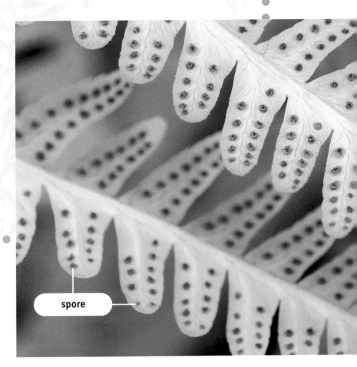

spore

Spores are clearly visible on the undersides of these fern fronds.

Development of seeds

Seeds develop inside fruits that protect the seeds and help to spread, or disperse, them. Seeds develop inside an ovary in the carpel. When seeds start to grow inside a flower, the petals are no longer needed so they die and fall from the plant. The ovary grows to form a fruit.

Seed dispersal

It is important to disperse seeds as far away from the parent as possible to avoid the new plant competing for resources such as light, water and nutrients. Some fruits are soft and fleshy, like plums or raspberries. When animals feed on the flesh, the animals sometimes drop the seeds on the

ANNUAL, BIANNUAL OR PERENNIAL

Annual plants such as poppies grow from seed, flower, spread their seeds and die in the same growing season. Biannual plants such as foxgloves complete their life cycle in two growing seasons. After the first year's growth, a biannual plant stores food in underground parts, rests over winter and then grows back in the following spring.

The biannual dies after producing flowers and seeds in the second growing season. Perennial plants live for two or more years. Most produce flowers and seeds every year, but some reproduce only once in their life cycle. For example, the talipot palm in India may live as long as 75 years before it flowers and fruits just once and then dies.

Corn poppies are annual plants and common weeds on agricultural land.

Sycamore seeds are small and light. Their wing-like structures allow them to spin as they fall from their parent tree and through the air. When they land, the seeds grow into new plants.

ground. Sometimes an animal swallows whole seeds, which pass through the animal's body and disperse where it leaves faeces on the ground. Some plants, such as hazels, have tough shells that help protect their seeds, or nuts, from being damaged by animals before they can germinate.

How long?

Some plants stay alive for longer than other plants. In general, the bigger and tougher a plant, the longer it lives. The oldest bristlecone pine growing in the deserts of the United States may be more than 4,900 years old. But delicate garden flowers may last just a few months (see box). The amount of time at each stage in a plant's life cycle differs widely, too. Arctic lupins usually live for about 10 years. But scientists have found lupin seeds estimated to be around 10,000 years old, preserved in the cold, dry air of an animal burrow. These seeds germinated within two days once they were put in warmer, wetter conditions.

The bristlecone pine lives longer than any other organism on Earth. Some trees are thought to be more than 5,000 years old.

CHAPTER 3

Invertebrate life cycles

Invertebrates are a varied group of animals without backbones. They range from simple sponges and worms to octopuses and insects. Scientists have identified more than two million species, which make up 98 per cent of the entire animal kingdom.

Invertebrate eggs

Most invertebrates lay small eggs that are pale or cream in colour. Some are so small that you can only see them under a microscope. A few are bigger, such as those of the stick insect, which are 1 cm long. Invertebrate eggs are usually small because they lay many eggs at one time. For example, the female Australian ghost moth lays more than 30,000 eggs in her lifetime. Invertebrates produce many eggs because they do not care for their young. As a result, many get eaten before they hatch and only a small proportion of the young grow into adults.

Many invertebrates lay their eggs on organisms that provide a source of food for the young when they hatch. Some wasps sting caterpillar prey to paralyse them.

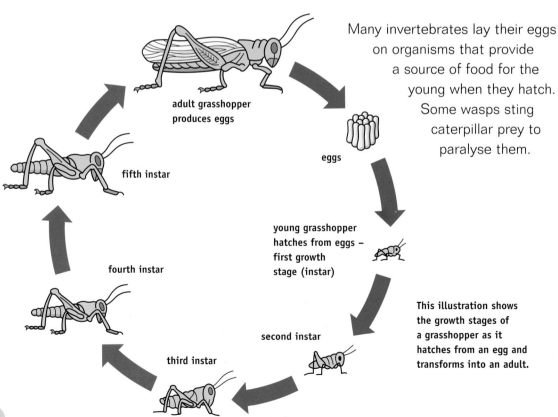

adult grasshopper produces eggs

eggs

fifth instar

fourth instar

third instar

second instar

young grasshopper hatches from eggs – first growth stage (instar)

This illustration shows the growth stages of a grasshopper as it hatches from an egg and transforms into an adult.

A butterfly lays its eggs on the underside of a leaf. The egg hatches into a caterpillar that will feed on the leaf.

Growing up

Invertebrates such as grasshoppers look like tiny versions of their parents when they hatch from their eggs. They gradually change into adults. Many invertebrates have hard outer skins, called exoskeletons, to support and protect their bodies. The young invertebrate sheds the exoskeleton as it grows. Other invertebrates, such as mussels, have shell exoskeletons. They secrete chemicals to enlarge their shells so they can get bigger inside.

Then they lay their eggs inside. Once they hatch, the wasp larvae eat the caterpillar from the inside out!

MOULTING

Invertebrates such as insects regularly shed their hard exoskeletons as they develop into adults. To prepare for moulting, the insect becomes inactive. The exoskeleton splits, and the insect crawls out. The insect's body expands with air and dries out to form a new, bigger exoskeleton. Most invertebrates moult about five times before becoming an adult. Others, such as silverfish, can moult up to 50 times.

A cicada sheds its skin as it grows into an adult. The new skin underneath is soft but hardens as it dries in the air.

Larvae to adult

When they hatch out of their eggs, invertebrates such as beetles and butterflies look completely different from the adults. The young undergo a dramatic transformation, called complete metamorphosis, to become adults.

There are four distinct stages to complete metamorphosis: egg, larva, pupa and adult. The larvae that hatch out of the eggs are caterpillars, grubs or maggots. They feed and grow very quickly. For example, a monarch butterfly larva can increase its weight by 2,000 times in just two weeks! When a larva is fully grown, it stops moving and seals itself inside a case called a pupa. Eventually, the pupa splits open and the fully formed adult emerges. New body parts such as wings unfold, harden and become ready to use.

Parasite life cycles

Some invertebrates live on or in the bodies of other animals, called hosts. These so-called parasites take in nutrients from their host without the need to find food themselves.

A caterpillar transforms into an adult monarch butterfly inside a protective shell called a chrysalis.

CARING FOR YOUNG

During the early stages of life, young invertebrates are vulnerable to predators and environmental factors such as the weather. Some invertebrates care for their young to ensure they have a better chance of survival. Others build a nest to keep the eggs and larvae in one place and protect them against predators. Social insects such as bees and ants live in large colonies with different members of the colony taking on different roles for the group. Workers protect, care and feed all the young produced by a single female, called a queen.

Ticks suck blood from their hosts. Tapeworms live inside the host's intestines and feed on what the host eats.

Young liver flukes live and grow inside snails and then leave the snail and stick onto grass leaves. They can remain like this until sheep eat the grass. The young flukes change into adults in the liver of the sheep, where they mate and produce eggs. The eggs leave the body of the sheep in its faeces. The eggs hatch, and the larvae move back into snails to complete the life cycle.

The pinworm is a parasitic roundworm that lives in the intestines of its human host.

Invertebrate reproduction

Most invertebrates reproduce sexually. Many simply release sperm and eggs into the water. Males of other invertebrates, including some crabs, locusts and scorpions, deposit sperm in protective capsules, which the female collects. Some male invertebrates deliver the sperm to the females. Male prawns pass their sperm into a pouch on the female where she then lays her eggs. Male octopuses use arms to place sperm into the body of the female.

Insects such as bees mate in the air as they fly. The female stores sperm to fertilise eggs over a long period of time. Some invertebrates, such as sea slugs, are hermaphrodites, which means one individual can make both sperm and

Sea slugs are hermaphrodites, which means they have both male and female sex organs. However, they usually reproduce by mating with other sea slugs.

eggs. A few invertebrates, such as aphids and coral, can reproduce asexually by dividing in two.

Life stages

Most invertebrates have short life cycles. They hatch, grow, reproduce and die in 12 months or less. Others, such as fruit flies, complete their life cycles in a matter of weeks. There are exceptions. Termite queens can live 40 years and lay thousands of eggs every day.

Coral reefs form when individual organisms called polyps bud. The colony members each secrete exoskeletons that fuse into the reef structure.

The length of each stage of the invertebrate's life cycle varies, too. The adult phase is often short compared to the larval stage. For example, a mayfly can live for a year as a larva but less than a day as an adult after it emerges from its pupa. The environment can also affect the length of life cycle.

For example, maggots develop into flies much quicker in warm, moist conditions. Similarly, cold or drought may delay the completion of life cycles. For example, locust eggs can tolerate dry desert conditions until the rains come and provide water for plants to grow and provide food for larvae.

MATING GAMES

Invertebrates need to mate to complete their life cycles, but this is easier for some species than others. In some species, such as the praying mantis (below), the female eats the male after mating. Scientists are not sure why the females do this. It may be because the smaller male is simply a handy source of food for the female and for the offspring she will have soon after. Female Mediterranean tarantula spiders that eat males after mating produce 30 per cent more eggs and stronger young than those females that do not.

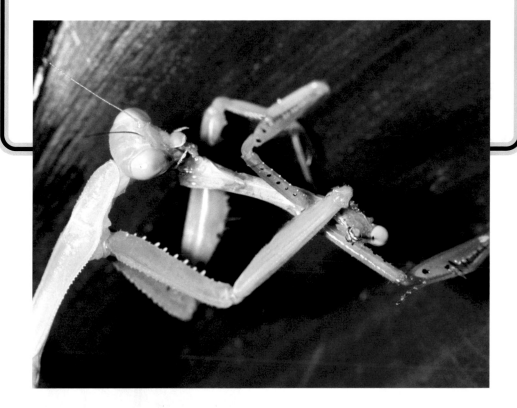

CHAPTER 4

Fish and amphibians

Fish and amphibians are vertebrates – animals with backbones. Fish and amphibians start their lives as eggs in water. Fish spend their entire live in the water, but amphibians switch between life in water and on the land. As amphibians develop in water they grow legs, allowing them to move on to land.

Eggs in water

Laying eggs in water has several advantages. The eggs do not dry out and the water keeps the eggs at a stable temperature so the developing young do not get too hot or cold. Most fish and amphibians lay hundreds or even millions of small, soft eggs. For example, the female turbot lays between 5 and 10 million tiny eggs at a time. Females of some species lay eggs several times each year for up to 30 years. When the tiny young hatch out of the eggs, they are vulnerable to predators. Laying lots of eggs is a tactic to ensure that at least some survive and develop into adults. Scientists think that only five out of every 2,000 frog eggs survive into adulthood.

Some fish lay eggs that float on the surface of the water. Others stick their eggs to plants or gravel on the river bed so they do not get washed away. Frogs and toads lay their eggs in sticky strings up to 1 metre long or in floating masses of jelly called frogspawn. Sharks and rays lay eggs in cases that protect the young fish inside.

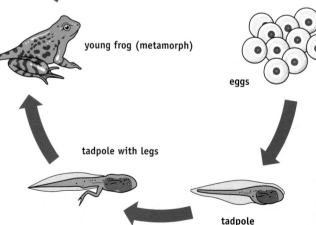

adult frog

young frog (metamorph)

eggs

tadpole with legs

tadpole

This illustration shows the reproductive stages of a typical frog life cycle, as the frog transforms from an egg into a tadpole and then into an adult.

A few amphibians lay their eggs out of water. Some tree frogs lay eggs in water that collects inside plants growing on trees. Others secrete a moist, sticky foam from their skin and lay their eggs in it.

Parental care

The females of most species of fish and amphibians hide their eggs under leaves or among gravel so predators do not eat them. The young usually hatch and grow up alone. Some fish and amphibians look after their young. The male midwife toad protects the eggs by carrying them on his back legs until they hatch. The female seahorse lays eggs in a pouch on the front of the male's body where they remain until they hatch. Some tilapia

The eggs of the yellow seahorse develop inside a brooding pouch on the male's body. The male carries the eggs for up to four weeks before he gives birth.

guard their eggs and protect the hatchlings by sucking them into their mouths.

EGGS ON THE INSIDE

Amphibians such as salamanders and caecilians and fish such as guppies do not hatch from eggs in water. Their embryos develop within eggs inside their mother's body. The eggs hatch inside, and the female gives birth to the young soon afterwards. These animals only give birth to a few young at a time. There is limited space inside the female's body, so she does not produce as many eggs. However, the eggs have a better chance of survival because they are better protected from predators. A few amphibians have a more unusual way of caring for eggs. The female Surinam toad sticks the eggs to her back, and skin grows over them until they are ready to hatch.

Fish changes

The time it takes for fish eggs to hatch varies among species. The young of some species hatch out after a day or two, but it can take up to five months for some sharks to develop. The young fish that hatch out are called fry. They are very small and cannot swim very well because their muscles and fins are not fully developed. At first, the fry feed on the yolk sac from the egg, which sticks to their stomach. Then they start to eat bits of food including plant material and insect eggs in the water. As the young fish grow, they begin to eat different foods. For example, tuna fry eat plankton. After three weeks, they have grown into miniature versions of the adult fish and eat small fish and prawns. The adults have big, bullet-shaped bodies and strong swimming muscles. They hunt in groups and eat bigger fish.

How fish reproduce

In most fish species, the females lay their eggs, and the males release sperm over them. Both parents swim away, leaving the eggs to hatch and the young to fend for themselves. The male stickleback fish prepares a nest for his eggs. He scrapes a hollow in the sand on the river bed, piles weeds on top and wriggles through the weeds to make a tunnel.

A male and female ghost pipefish swim together as they mate. The eggs develop inside a brooding pouch on the female's body.

SALMON MIGRATION

The migration of the Pacific salmon is one of the miracles of nature. These fish hatch and spend the first part of their lives in freshwater. Then they migrate thousands of kilometres to the ocean, where they spend their adult lives, which can range from six months to as long as seven years. When the salmon reach sexual maturity, they return to the freshwater streams in which they hatched to reproduce. The fish face many threats during the migration, such as hungry bears and the nets of fishermen. After spawning, the Pacific salmon swim to shore and die, which completes their life cycle.

The male displays to the females to encourage them to lay eggs inside his nest. He then releases his sperm over them.

In the dark depths of the ocean, male fish find females using scent. When the male anglerfish finds a female, he bites and holds on to her underside. His body then connects with the female's body. The male releases his sperm as soon as the female releases her eggs. Some fish mate to reproduce. The fins of male sharks and topminnows are shaped like tubes to pass sperm inside the female.

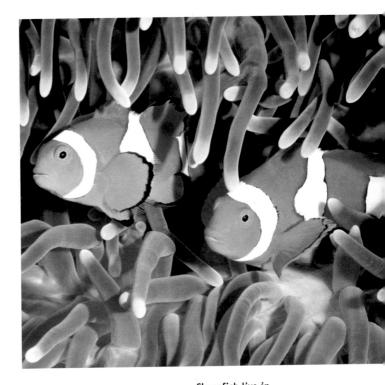

Clownfish live in small groups inside a sea anemone. The clownfish is immune to the toxic poison produced by the sea anemone and is therefore protected from predators.

Same sex

A few fish species are hermaphrodites, which means they can act as males and females – either at the same time or at different times in their lives. Clownfish live in groups with one large female, one small mature male and several immature males. If the female dies, the mature male turns into a female and one of the immature males becomes the mature male. The Amazon molly is unusual because the female reproduces asexually from her own unfertilised eggs.

Frogs and toads

Most amphibians hatch in the water but live on land as adults. Amphibians such as frogs and toads undergo a dramatic transformation, called metamorphosis, when they are ready to live on land. Frogs and toads that hatch from eggs are called tadpoles. They have tails to help them swim. Most have feathery structures, called gills, to breathe underwater and sucking mouths to feed on plants.

As the tadpoles grow into frogs and toads, their jaws change so the adults can catch animal food such as insects. Frogs and toads develop lungs to breathe air. The tail is gradually reabsorbed into the body, and finally the amphibian grows legs to climb on to the land.

Salamanders and newts

Other amphibians do not undergo such a dramatic change. Red-spotted newts have a three-stage life cycle. The female lays her eggs under water. The green larvae eventually hatch and live underwater, breathing using their feathery gills. In the next stage of development, the larvae become bright red-orange and lose their gills. They grow lungs to breathe air and live on land. After two or three years, the newts change into brown, spotted adults with gills and a powerful finned tail. They return to the water and stay there for the rest of their lives. Some tailed amphibians spend all their lives in the water. Giant salamanders and amphibians called hellbenders live in fast-flowing rivers and streams.

Reproduction and death

Amphibians often lay their eggs in the same ponds in which they hatched themselves. Some newts migrate up to 10 kilometres to reach their breeding ponds. Male frogs and toads often croak to attract females. They expand the skin in their throats to make the call as loud as possible. When a male finds a female, he will usually grip onto her body, ready to fertilise her eggs.

The larva of a frog is called a tadpole. It lives in the water and absorbs oxygen using feathery structures called gills.

Male salamanders and newts often change colour to attract females during the breeding season. Some display to females by lashing their tails and showing off the crests on their backs.

Adult frogs spend their lives on the land but return to the water to breed.

Amphibians return to the same breeding pond year after year. Unfortunately, many ponds are being drained. Combined with the threat from predators, this means many amphibians may only live for one or two years at most. The longest living amphibians are giant salamanders. They have no natural predators and can live for several decades in remote mountain rivers.

ETERNAL YOUTH

Some salamanders appear to stay in their larval stage and never develop into adults. The axolotl keeps the feathery gills it had when it was a larva. Although it resembles a larva, the axolotl is an adult that can reproduce. Its gills help it breathe in the damp caves in which it lives.

CHAPTER 5

Reptiles and birds

Reptiles are vertebrates with scales and include animals such as crocodiles, snakes and turtles. Birds are vertebrates with feathers and range in size from hummingbirds to ostriches. Both birds and reptiles reproduce by laying eggs. The young generally hatch out as smaller versions of the adults and complete their life cycles on land.

Tough eggs

The eggs of reptiles are usually white with soft, leathery shells. The eggs of birds have hard shells. Eggs protect the developing young from damage and seal in water so the embryos do not dry out in hot weather. The eggs contain food in the form of a yolk, and the embryo sits in a sac of watery fluid. The shell of the egg is porous, which means it is covered with tiny holes – about 7,000 in a chicken eggshell. Air passes through the holes so the embryo can breathe. When the young reptile or bird is ready to hatch, it uses an egg tooth to bite through the egg and hatch.

Keeping eggs warm

The embryos of reptiles and birds can only develop inside the eggs if they are kept warm. This is called incubation. Birds and reptiles incubate their eggs in different ways.

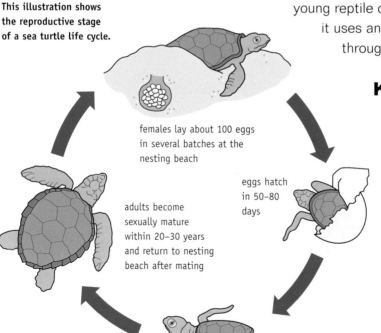

This illustration shows the reproductive stage of a sea turtle life cycle.

females lay about 100 eggs in several batches at the nesting beach

eggs hatch in 50–80 days

adults become sexually mature within 20–30 years and return to nesting beach after mating

nursery stage – young turtles live in open ocean for between 5 and 20 years

A spiny softshell turtle emerges from its egg. The hatchling looks like a miniature version of the adult turtle.

Most birds keep their eggs in a nest, and one or both parents sit on the eggs to incubate them. The adults have a patch of bare skin, called a brood patch, to transfer body heat to the eggs. The bird plucks its feathers to reveal the brood patch, or the feathers fall out naturally. The feathers grow back over the brood patch after the eggs hatch.

Most reptiles usually abandon their eggs after laying them, so other incubation methods are used. Female alligators lay their eggs in mounds of leaves, which release heat as they rot. After mating, some female turtles dig holes in sand or soil, lay their eggs in them and cover the eggs to hide them from predators.

INVESTIGATE:
Egg strength

YOU WILL NEED:
4 eggshells, table, books

The curved shape of an egg spreads the weight of an object placed on the egg over its whole surface. This helps prevent it cracking, for example when a parent incubates the egg. Test the strength of a chicken egg by placing the halves of four empty eggshells on a table, rounded side up, and spaced in a rectangle about the size of a book. Then gently balance books, one at a time, on top of the shells. You may be surprised by how many books you can add before the eggshells crack.

Reptile young

When they hatch, young reptiles look like miniature versions of their parents. They are fully equipped to find food and look after themselves. For example, young rattlesnakes are born with the ability to hunt. They have as much venom as an adult, so they can paralyse prey before swallowing it. Young reptiles have scaly skin – or shells in the case of turtles and tortoises. Scales and shells protect reptiles from heat and predators. The thickness of the scales or shell increases with age, however few reptiles survive their first year of life.

Mating

When reptiles mature into adults they can mate. Males usually display to the females to attract them to mate. This is called courtship. Geckos use mating calls to attract mates. Male chameleons attract females by changing colour, using tiny dots of pigment under the surface

The sex of a crocodile depends on the temperature of the egg when it was incubated.

of the skin. Iguana courtship is more active. The male nods his head, raises the frill of spines on his head or back and spreads and closes his dewlap – a flap of skin under his throat. Unlike amphibians and fish, a male reptile has a penis and uses it to put sperm inside the female's body.

Returning to land

Most reptiles are oviparous. Even those that live in water return to lay their eggs on land, otherwise water would seep into the porous eggs and drown the young. Female turtles lay their eggs on the same beaches on which they hatched themselves, many years before.

Boas and vipers are viviparous snakes. Females hold the fertilised eggs inside their bodies and give birth to 'live' young.

REPTILE SKIN

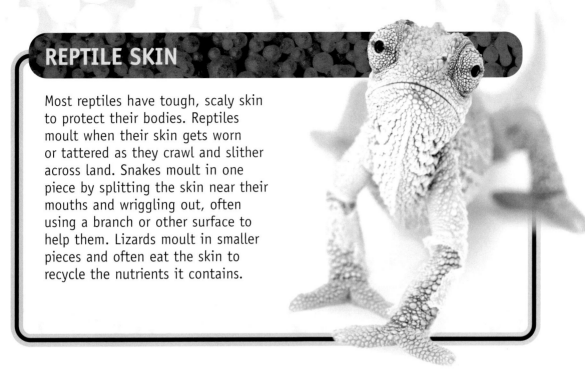

Most reptiles have tough, scaly skin to protect their bodies. Reptiles moult when their skin gets worn or tattered as they crawl and slither across land. Snakes moult in one piece by splitting the skin near their mouths and wriggling out, often using a branch or other surface to help them. Lizards moult in smaller pieces and often eat the skin to recycle the nutrients it contains.

Boas can live up to 40 years. However, turtles and tortoises are the most long-lived of all the reptiles – some can live for 180 years. Loggerhead turtles may take 25 years to develop from a hatchling into an adult. Some reptiles, such as side-blotched lizards, are annual species. They usually complete their life cycle and die within one year.

A newly hatched turtle crawls along the sand towards the sea. If it survives into adulthood, the turtle can expect to live for up to 80 years.

Nesting birds

Most birds lay their eggs in nests. These range in size from the tiny cup-shaped nests of hummingbirds, which are lined with feathers and spiders' webs, to to stick nests several metres wide made by eagles. Parents care for their young for many weeks because the chicks cannot survive on their own. The eyes of the chicks are covered with skin, and they have few feathers to keep warm. Parents use up a lot of energy feeding the chicks and keeping them warm as they develop. When the young birds grow flight feathers, they no longer need the care of their parents. Some birds, including blue jays, live in groups in which several young adults raise the chicks in groups called crèches.

VARIETY OF EGGS

Egg range in size from the bean-sized hummingbird egg to the giant ostrich egg, which weighs about 3 kilograms. Some birds lay many eggs while others lay a single egg. Most are similar in shape to a hen's egg. Razorbills and guillemots lay eggs that are very pointed at one end. These birds lay their eggs on narrow rocky ledges. If the eggs are accidentally knocked, the pointed shape means they will roll in a small circle rather than fall into the sea below.

A stork raises its young in a large stick nest built on top of a nesting platform such as a tree or telegraph pole.

Some birds do not make nests. Emperor penguins live in the Antarctic where it is incredibly cold. There are no nesting materials in the frozen wasteland, so male penguins incubate their eggs by resting them on their feet and tucking them under skin pouches below the stomach. Other birds, such as nightjars, lay eggs with mottled patterns so they blend in with the colour of the ground. This camouflages the eggs so predators cannot spot them.

Breeding season

Birds usually breed when the weather is good and there is lots of food for their young. For example, tits and warblers breed in the spring and summer when there insect food is plentiful. Males often use colourful feathers and dramatic courtship displays to attract females.

Perhaps the most spectacular example is the tail feathers of the peacock. The male shakes his tail feathers like a giant fan to attract mates. Birds often pair for life but usually live separate lives outside the breeding season. During the next breeding season, birds greet, court and mate with the same partner once more.

Long lives

Generally, seabirds and other large birds live longer than smaller birds that live in colder regions on the land. Small birds are more vulnerable to temperature changes, and there are more predators on land than at sea. Birds from tropical regions live longer because the climate is warm and there is lots of food to eat. The longest-living birds include parrots called cockatoos (75 years) and ostriches (40 years).

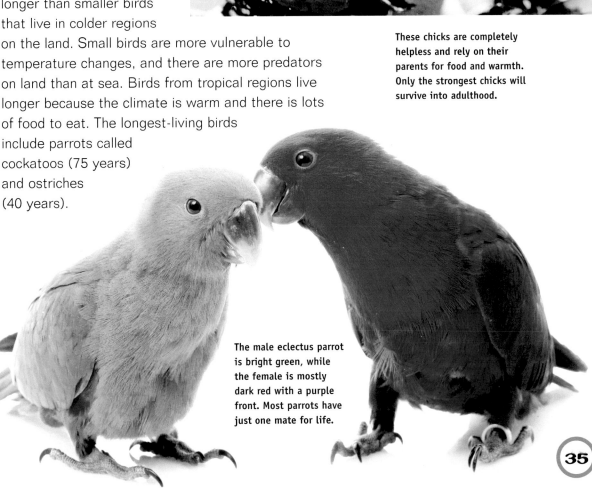

These chicks are completely helpless and rely on their parents for food and warmth. Only the strongest chicks will survive into adulthood.

The male eclectus parrot is bright green, while the female is mostly dark red with a purple front. Most parrots have just one mate for life.

CHAPTER 6

Mammal life cycles

Mammals give birth to live young, and the females feed them with milk produced by their mammary glands. Young mammals are cared for by at least one of their parents during the first vulnerable stages of their life cycle.

In the uterus

Almost all mammals develop as embryos inside their mother's womb, or uterus. The uterus expands as the embryo develops and grows. Mammals feed their young through an organ called a placenta. The placenta transfers nutrients from the mother's blood, through the umbilical cord, to the embryo's blood. The food supply from the placenta is not limited like the yolk of an egg. The placenta also removes waste from the embryo. Mammals can develop safely inside their mother's uterus for much longer than oviparous animals can remain inside eggs.

Hamsters develop inside their mother for three weeks, lions develop in 15 weeks and elephants develop in 22 months. The advantage of such a long gestation is that the young are more developed when they are born. Some herbivores, including deer and giraffes, are born ready to run when faced with danger.

This illustration shows the reproductive stages of a typical mouse life cycle.

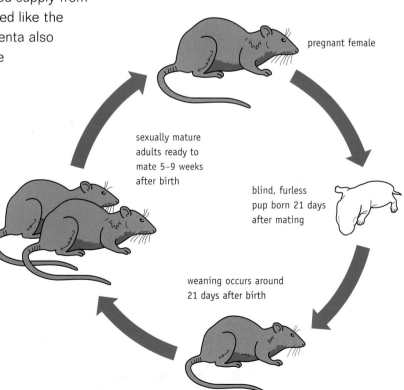

pregnant female

sexually mature adults ready to mate 5–9 weeks after birth

blind, furless pup born 21 days after mating

weaning occurs around 21 days after birth

A young giraffe is so well developed at birth that it can run a few hours after being born.

Mammals with pouches

Marsupials are mammals that do not feed their young through a placenta. Instead, the female gives birth to young at a very early stage in their development. The tiny offspring cannot survive in the outside world, so they complete their development in a pouch on their mother's body. Inside the pouch, the young marsupial latches onto its mother's nipple to drink milk, sleep and grow. A newborn kangaroo is called a joey. The joey spends between six and 11 months inside the pouch before it is ready to live on its own.

A female kangaroo gives birth to one young kangaroo, which develops inside a pouch on her body.

EGG-LAYING MAMMALS

Monotremes are a small group of unusual mammals. Unlike other mammals, these animals – the duck-billed platypus and two kinds of echidnas (spiny anteaters) – lay eggs. Like other mammals, however, the bodies of these animals are covered in fur, and the female feeds her young with milk. After mating, the female duck-billed platypus lays two or three soft-shelled eggs in a waterside burrow and incubates them for up to two weeks. A female echidna lays a single leathery egg in a pouch on her stomach. Ten days later, the young echidna hatches and remains in the pouch for about six weeks.

Caring parents

Parental care is vital when mammals are young. Many young mammals are born with no fur, their eyes are closed and they are helpless. Female mammals bear a smaller number of offspring than most other animals, because the level of parental care is much higher. The mother feeds her young with milk, and one or both parents keep them warm and protect them from danger. This level of care creates strong bonds between parents and their young.

A vulnerable baby baboon is protected and tended to by different members of its family group, not just its mother.

Early years

All mammals stay with their mother until they are weaned, which means they have stopped feeding on their mother's milk. At this stage, most young mammals have developed fully formed teeth so they can eat solid food. Many young mammals stay with their family and learn useful skills to help fend for themselves. For example, lion and tiger cubs learn to fight and hunt by playing with their siblings. Many mammals live in large social groups and only leave when they are ready to have their own young.

Changes into adults

Young mammals often look like smaller versions of their parents, but they do change in appearance as they become adults. For example, the fur of young mammals is often a different colour from the fur of the adults. Young baboons have

MAMMAL MILK

Milk is a complete food for young mammals. Different mammals produce different kinds of milk. Whale and seal milk is high in fat so the young can grow a thick layer of blubber to keep them warm in the cold ocean. Young hares drink milk that is high in sugar and protein to give them lots of energy, because the female feeds them only once a day.

Kittens suckle milk from their mother's mammary glands. All mammals feed their young in this way.

dark fur, which later changes to the lighter adult colour. Cheetah cubs have long, spotted hair, which acts as camouflage when the cubs are young and vulnerable.

As young mammals become adults, differences between the sexes become obvious. Male lions grow a thick mane, and some female chimps develop large, puffy red bottoms. These changes show that the animals are mature and ready to mate.

A male lion develops a thick mane of hair when he reaches adulthood, which signals to lionesses that he is ready to mate.

Mammal mating

Mammals mate to produce offspring. Most mammals mate in a breeding season. Some mammals, such as chimps and lions, live in social groups in which there are always males to mate with females. There may be one dominant male in the group that mates with all the mature females, while the younger males do not mate. The dominant male usually displays to the other males to show off his strength and fitness. For example, a dominant gorilla stands on his back legs, beats his chest and screams at the other males.

Adult males usually join up with females in a herd of elephants in the breeding season.

Ready to mate

In most mammals, males and females live apart except during the breeding season. Female tigers roar and produce strong-smelling urine to signal to the males that they are ready to mate. The females of some mammal species, such as elephants and humpback whales, live in groups, while the males live separately.

Male elephants become aggressive before mating, charging and trumpeting with their trunks. They may even fight for the right to mate with the females. Male humpback whales sing complex songs, which they repeat for hours on end. Females can hear the songs from

INVESTIGATE:
Human life cycle

Investigate the life cycles of different generations of people. You could choose members of your own family, such as grandparents, parents, aunts and uncles. Look at family records, photo albums and other sources to find out about the different stages of their lives. When were they born? How old were they when they had children? How old were they when they died? You could present the data on a family tree and include photos. People live longer today than in the past, and they also have children later. Can you think why this might be?

up to 10 kilometres away and choose to mate with the male that sings the most complex songs. Only about 3 per cent of all mammals are monogamous, which means one male mates with one female through their adult lives.

Old age

The life span of mammals varies according to species. A small mammal, such as a shrew, may live for under a year, while horses can live for 20 years and elephants for up to 70 years. Due to advances in medicine, human beings are the longest-living mammals. A few people have lived to reach more than 110 years old.

Like any other animal, mammals become weaker as they grow older. They get thin, their muscles shrink and they are more vulnerable to illness and injury. Since older mammals are less active, they may not be able to hunt and catch food as they once did.

Chimpanzees live in complex communities consisting of groups of males, females and their young and groups of both sexes. One or more dominant males controls the chimp community.

41

Seed to seeds

In this activity you will study the life cycle of a sunflower under different growing conditions. Plant a sunflower seed and watch the plant grow and produce flowers and seeds in the summer. Sunflower seeds are large and easy to handle, and they germinate quickly and easily. The flowers will grow best outside in the summer, so plan to plant your seeds early in the spring.

You will need:
- 4 flowerpots
- 8 sunflower seeds
- compost
- sand
- cling film

1. Plant up four flowerpots, each with two sunflower seeds: fill three pots with potting compost and one with sand. Push a stick into the pot to make a hole about 2 cm deep for each seed. Water the soil to make it moist. Cover the pots with cling film to prevent water loss.

2. Vary the conditions by putting the pots in different positions. Put one compost pot and the sand pot on a sunny windowsill. Put the second compost pot in the shade and the final compost pot in cool place. Check the pots regularly to ensure that the compost or sand is not too dry. Can you predict which growing conditions will encourage the quickest germination?

3. Remove the cling film when the seeds have germinated after about two weeks. Check to see which of the two seedlings in each pot is the weakest. Pull it out to leave one strong seedling in each pot. Put all the pots back on a sunny windowsill. Water them regularly.

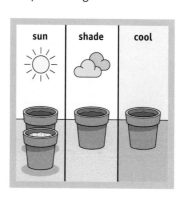

4. From early summer stand the pots outside during the daytime to 'harden off' your sunflowers. This means get them used to the cooler temperatures outside.

5. When the plants are about 10 to 15 cm tall (and when you are sure the danger of overnight frost has passed), plant the seedlings in their pots into the garden. The roots should have grown through the peat. Can you see the roots of the sunflower planted in the sand pot? If you do not have a garden, plant your seedlings into big pots of compost. Vary the conditions by planting or standing the sunflowers in two different positions – one that is always shady and the other in full sunlight.

6. By late summer the plants should be tall and flowering. Compare the heights of the different plants and the position of the flower head, which should be facing towards the sun.

7. When the flower head droops downwards you can collect the seeds from it. Count the seeds to see how many have grown from a single seed. Store the seeds in a dark, dry place. You can grow more sunflowers the following spring to continue the sunflower's life cycle.

Glossary

amphibian Cold-blooded vertebrate that reproduces in water from soft eggs.

asexual Reproduction without sex cells.

camouflage Hiding by blending in with the surroundings.

cell Basic building block of all living organisms.

cold-blooded Term used to describe animals that cannot control their own body temperature.

decompose Break down into chemicals. Dead organisms decompose at the end of their life cycles.

differentiate When less specialised cells become specialised cells, often in tissues such as muscles and nerves.

DNA Deoxyribonucleic acid, the chemical from which chromosomes are made.

egg Female sex cell.

embryo Organism in its early stages of growth.

gene Sequence of DNA that carries one piece of genetic information.

germinate/germination When a seed starts to grow.

gestation Period when a developing embryo grows inside its mother.

gills Feathery structures used by some animals to breathe under water.

habitat Place where an organism lives. There are many different habitats in the world, ranging from mountain tops to the ocean depths.

incubate Keep egg warm to ensure the embryo develops inside.

insect Invertebrate that has three pairs of legs and a segmented body (head, thorax and abdomen) as an adult.

insulate To slow or block the movement of sound, heat or electricity.

invertebrates Animals that do not have backbones.

larva Stage of growth of some insects after hatching from the egg. Most larvae are wingless and resemble a caterpillar or grub.

mammal Warm-blooded vertebrate covered with hair or fur; females give birth to live young and feed young with milk from the mammary glands.

metamorphosis Complete change of physical form from a larva (such as a tadpole) into an adult (such as a frog).

moult Periodically shed skin or other outer covering.

niche An organism's particular role within its habitat.

nutrients Substances that organisms need to live.

organism Any living thing, such as an animal, plant, bacterium or fungus.

parasite Organism that lives on or inside another organism.

photosynthesis Process by which green plants trap energy from sunlight and use it to make food from carbon dioxide and water.

pollen Grains that contain the male reproductive cells of a seed plant.

pollinate Transfer pollen from the flower of one plant to another plant of the same species.

predator Animal that hunts another animal for food.

prey Animal hunted for food.

pupa Stage of growth when an insect larva metamorphoses into an adult.

reproduce To have offspring.

reptile Cold-blooded vertebrate that usually lays eggs to bear young. Reptiles are covered with scales or plates and breathe using lungs.

scales Overlapping or interlocking bony plates that form a protective layer over the skin of reptiles and fish.

species All the organisms that can mate with one another and produce fertile offspring.

sexual reproduction When sperm fertilises an egg.

sperm Male sex cell that can usually move to an egg to fertilise it.

spore Reproductive unit of some plants and fungi.

thorax Middle section of an insect's body that bears wings and legs.

uterus Part of a female mammal's body where an embryo develops (also called the womb).

vertebrates Animals that have backbones.

warm-blooded Animals that can maintain their body temperature using the energy from their food.

Further information

WEBSITES TO VISIT

Find out how we develop from eggs into adult human beings at:
www.sciencemuseum.org.uk/exhibitions/lifecycle/index.asp

Learn all about animal reproduction and metamorphosis at:
www.saburchill.com/chapters/chap0031.html

Find out more about pollination and pollinators at:
www.mbgnet.net/bioplants/pollination.html

For information on the ways in which organisms reproduce asexually visit:
http://users.rcn.com/jkimball.ma.ultranet/BiologyPages/A/AsexualReproduction.html

Index